The Walt McDonald First-Book Series in Poetry

Robert A. Fink, *editor*

The Glad Hand of God Points Backwards

Texas Tech University Press

Introduction by Robert A. Fink

POEMS

RACHEL
MENNIES

The Glad Hand
of God Points
Backwards

This book is typeset in Minion Pro. The paper used in this book meets the minimum requirements of ANSI/NISO Z39.48-1992 (R1997). ∞

Designed by Ashley Beck
Cover photograph/illustration by Ashley Beck

Library of Congress Cataloging-in-Publication Data

Mennies, Rachel, author.
        [Poems. Selections]
        The Glad Hand of God Points Backwards : Poems / Rachel Mennies ; Introduction by Robert A. Fink.
                pages cm. — (Walt McDonald First-Book Series)
                Summary: "Twenty-third winner of the Walt McDonald First-Book Prize in Poetry."—Provided by publisher
                ISBN 978-0-89672-854-7 (hardback) I. Title.
                PS3613.E4916A6 2014
                811'.6—dc23   2013050925

Printed in Canada

14 15 16 17 18 19 20 21 22 / 9 8 7 6 5 4 3 2 1

Texas Tech University Press
Box 41037 | Lubbock, Texas 79409-1037 USA
800.832.4042 | ttup@ttu.edu | www.ttupress.org

For Eve Schönwetter Mennies, Bernard B. Mennies,
Beverly Provisor Hoffman, and Howard Edgar Hoffman:
"A man whose very name is laughter—heh! heh! heh!"

I said, I'll move back a little, as at an exhibition,
to see the whole picture. And
I haven't stopped moving back.

Time is as light as froth,
the heavy sediment stays in us forever.

Yehuda Amichai, "In the Morning It Was Still Night"

Contents

Introduction

And these words that I ["the Lord our God"]
command you today shall be on your heart.
You shall teach them diligently to your children,
and shall talk of them when you sit in your house,
and when you walk by the way,
and when you lie down, and when you rise.
You shall bind them as a sign on your hand,
and they shall be as frontlets between your eyes.
You shall write them on the doorposts
of your house and on your gates.

Deuteronomy 6: 6-9 (ESV)

Rachel Mennies's delightfully enigmatic title of her poetry book *The
Glad Hand of God Points Backwards* suggests a deliberately ambiguous,
ironic interpretation of God's hand that protects, that judges, that points
to history, heritage, the promises made to Adam, Noah, Abraham, Isaac,
and Jacob, the law meted out to Moses and the children of Israel. God of
the Garden of Eden. God of the *Shema*. This *Thou Shalt* and *Thou Shalt
Not* hand of God, however, is also a *glad* hand, welcoming hand—one
that "accepts / the muddle of our lives," a God who "holds / nobody
responsible," who says, "'As you wish,'" and then "retreats into the sunset
alone" ("The Jewish Woman in America, 2010"). *Glad hand* also con-
notes what could be a less-than-sincere gesture: "For my thoughts are
not your thoughts, / neither are your ways my ways, declares the Lord"
(Isaiah 55:8, ESV). There will be no pat, no comfortable answers in this
collection of poetry.

The Bible, ancient texts, theological and historical renderings,
movies, have offered no end of possible interpretations of the nature of
God, both loving and awful (awe-filled), terrible. There have been many
depictions of the conflagrations falling upon God's chosen people, the
Jews, so what does Rachel Mennies's poetry book offer that we haven't
already read or seen? This is the question I asked as I began reading *The*

Glad Hand of God Points Backwards. This is the question I have asked of all the Walt McDonald First-Book Prize in Poetry manuscripts I have read since 1996. Isn't this the question we all ask of literature? Why should we read this book? What will it teach us about ourselves, about "what it means human" (Bernard Malamud, *Idiots First*)? Of course, each reader will have to answer this question for herself, but for me the answer comes through Rachel Mennies's persona looking back upon her people's history, her heritage both historical and personal, a matriarchal heritage of Law that may not provide comforting guidance for a contemporary woman. And, yes, hers is primarily a *matriarchal* heritage, stories preserved, passed down mother to daughter, grandmother to granddaughter, instructing each generation what it means to be the Jewish woman.

For those of us who are neither Jewish, nor female, what can this book teach us about ourselves? In several interviews, novelist and short fiction writer Bernard Malamud said everybody is a Jew, but we don't know it. This sentiment is underscored by Malamud in his short story "Angel Levine," when in the concluding sentence, Manichevitz rushes into their apartment to declare joyfully to his wife: "'A wonderful thing, Fanny. . . . Believe me, there are Jews everywhere.'" Malamud offered a possible interpretation of his comment: history sooner or later, treats all people as Jews. Don't we all feel displaced? Don't we all suffer and at times take sardonic comfort from what Malamud's rabbinical student in "The Magic Barrel" drew consolation after his dark night/week of the soul, acknowledging "that he was a Jew and that a Jew suffered."

The Glad Hand of God Points Backwards reconstructs what it means *Jewish*, what it means *Jewish woman*, from Eve to the present, working backwards—Jewish grandmother, mother, wife, lover, teenager, child, living and passing down "the text of all stories" read by matriarchs "to their children at nightfall" ("Matriarch"). The question is *how* to reconstruct these stories, their "trinkets," "household objects," fragile relics excavated "whole / from an earth still kind / to its company" ("How to Make Yourself Remembered"). God's glad hand points to the past, the genesis of what becomes the present, the beginning of multiplication—"God's unscientific tale-telling, / the stories of stories, books / of books, myths of survival," the earth, our ethnic and blood-tied families multiplying "with creatures, beautiful as they were dumb," their silence demanding an excavator to unearth their collective and individual stories ("Learning to Multiply").

The task becomes how to select "the right stories to tell" and how to orchestrate them *right*, reconstructing the stories the way the poet wants ("The Storytelling Disease"). These "tiny histories" multiply generationally, creating "communes of myth" as we "dwell in the stories we must always learn to tell" ("The Gossips"), each of us "held in the mouth / of . . . [our] . . . family narrative," poets growing up "to write down the truth / and the lies together" to read "the past first" ("I Don't Know the Story, But I Can Tell the Story"). Each page must stay "in the right order" ("The Memory of the Witness"), plotting a complex heritage—"some sour / blackness against the yellow sun, grit / in the gift of sustenance" ("Huevos for Seder, viii").

These are tales preserved and passed down by women of faith whose heads are covered in public, "their skirts / making dark mysteries / of their legs," both themselves and their stories "the fabric of inaccessible glory," this paradoxical heritage conflicting their young, contemporary granddaughters wresting "a path without limits, two strong / and willful legs to bare to a street full of eyes" ("The Jewish Woman in America, 2010"). The book becomes a quest for a personal identity conjoined to and separate from a heritage prescribed by God's Law, his covenant with a people he has chosen and sometimes seems to abandon.

Rachel Mennies's backward view groups the poems in *The Glad Hand of God Points Backwards* into five sections, which seem an archeological dig excavating the past to display its consequences for the young, Jewish woman in contemporary America, seemingly "forever stuck / in self-reflection" ("The Creation of Temple Beth Sholom"). The book's persona thinks it easier than she anticipated to "shrug off" her European grandmother's Jewish identity, what has been the persona's "warm jacket," but she discovers that underneath the jacket is "the slow, / naked heart / of shame," the lineage of Jewish grandmothers and great-grandmothers bequeathing "their same / old matriarch hips, / same balled / matriarch fists" ("Huevos for Seder, v").

Section I, "The Glad Hand," introduces the persona's generational and personal heritage—"prayers / old as a thousand matriarchs, made / from symbols of mystery" ("Learning to Multiply"). These formidable matriarchs "lived thick with God's ironies" ("Matriarch"), a God from whom the young persona believes she can wrest her own path, separate from the matriarchs', "a path without limits" ("The Jewish Woman in America, 2010"). The following four sections suggest otherwise.

Section II is entitled "The Glass Overcoat." These fifteen poems develop the persona's personal and family connection to the most recent of Jewish holocausts: the horrors for European Jews targeted for Hitler's genocidal pogroms and death camps. The focus is on the stories told by the persona's European grandmother, who escaped Nazi Germany and came to New York and later Philadelphia; it also spotlights the persona's grandfather who witnessed the horrors of the camps as an American soldier, "the future / . . . smudged, undeniable," causing him to wring his "tired hands, unprepared / to touch babies with [his] war-ruined palms" ("The Will of God"). The persona's great-grandmother sold every-thing of value to save her daughter, purchase passage to New York. The businessmen "who stayed behind / one week, two weeks more" became the "stylish" horror: "coins from fillings / and wedding rings, the soap, the wigs, lamp / after lamp to light a thousand decorated homes" ("How Grandmother Paid Her Passage to New York"). And God said, "It's not so easy" ("Grandfather Loses His First Wife, i") keeping "His promises" ("Grandfather Loses His First Wife, iii"), "our God, the / collector of stories / and bodies" ("Grandfather Loses His First Wife, ii"). And those who escaped had to live with "the guilt: / the weight, the backbend-ing weight / of survival" ("The Jewish Profession"). A year, years, later "the eye of God opens, unblinking," the Yahrzeit candle flickering "on the windowsill, making / constellations of all our deaths" ("Yahrzeit," Section II).

Section III, "The Book, Open," explains how to tell the family's story, always "the past first" ("I Don't Know the Story, But I Can Tell the Story"), the Jewish poem, new for each family, the same for each family ("How to Make a Jewish Poem"). The stories maybe true, maybe "remembered wrong," someone else's stories mixed with the storyteller's tales told by a "synagogue yenta," true nonetheless ("The Story telling Disease"), stories shared at the Passover meal along with the mourners' prayer and a joke told against the horrors of history, clutching our sides, laughing "until we weep" ("The Joke").

"Elijah," the title of section IV, relocates the persona in Spain, her *madre Madrileña* complicating even further the persona's quest for a self independent from her heritage. Is the persona Jewish? American? German? Madrileña assures the persona that no matter where she resides, she is Jewish—nationalism an "unscalable wall, that darkened, / padlocked home" ("Huevos for Seder, ii"). She inherits "the menacing map entire," living "lost, in each nation of sand" ("Huevos for Seder, ii"). In Spain, like Madrileña, she slurps the Seder egg raw. In America, the egg is eaten hardboiled. Either way, "the egg is commentary: symbol / of a temple's destruction," leaving "the taste / of sulfur" ("Huevos for Seder, vii").

Section V, "The Jewish Woman in America," concludes the backwards look, examining the consequences of the Jewish woman's heritage for contemporary American teenage girls and young women. The previous section introduced the persona to the "men of Spain," their "stadium hungers," a hunger shared by the persona, ignoring the Jewish matriarchs—"mothers / still on Eastern Standard time, / constantly living in the past" ("Huevos for Seder, vi"). The young persona can defiantly say, "*Good*" or say "nothing / at all," taking these sons of Catholic, "sleeping mothers," a "whole and new" experience ("Huevos for Seder, vi"). The final section begins by looking back to the persona and her sister as children playing dress-up, taking turns dressing in the "hand-me-down" bridal gown found in the basement. And the imagined husband? Jewish. "*What other kind of man / is there?*" the sister asks ("Solomon").

The contemporary Jewish teenage girl in America, however, considers "*The God of History*" to be "dangerous," a "brute teacher," who seems to deny young women "pleasure, that quiet subtext, that patient search against / our partners' sweaty brows" ("Amidah for Teenage Girls"). This desire seems to reject the Jewish marriage tradition, in this case the tradition of the persona's grandmother's generation, preferring the "laughing man," his desire "an open, flattened hand," not "the grinding fist, the blanched knuckle" ("How to Make a Jewish Marriage, 1949"). An honorable Jewish wife's "story / begins: the book open like supplicant palms" ("How to Make a Jewish Marriage, 1949").

Taking her first Gentile, the young persona hopes for her own Hanukah miracle, but she cannot deny her "'thinking so much,'" her "worries of my great-aunts, / their consonant names" ("First Gentile"). In learning the "grinding gears" of her desire, she learns "nothing" ("To Those Still Godless"). And if (when) she marries a Gentile, how will their children be raised—Jewish or Christian? What will be the consequence for the persona, for her sister, and all other contemporary, young American, Jewish women—the "ones who mourn / a change, then change; / the ones who must" ("How Will You Raise Your Children?").

The consequence for the persona's younger sister is bulimia ("My Sister the Diviner") and "a calculus / of her fear"—obsessive-compulsive disorder ("My Sister the Abacus"). The consequence for the persona after she marries a Christian is that because both she and her husband "shout *Abraham!* / with equal weight in both / their prayerful mouths," their families, "their tribesmen count / the flock apart—as *hers*, as *his*" ("A Creature of All Scripture"). And having willfully sought her own path, desiring the sensual peach of rapture, peach—"the very taste / of sin," having satisfied herself, she will come to God "pitted, come to him / finished, made rotten by" her "sweet time in his sun" ("Rapture"). So, as the final poem in the collection, "The Jewish Woman Remembers Deuteronomy 6:6-9," the Jewish *Shema*, reveals, the persona still cries "for God in worship, later / in bed, witness to the power of giving / up our power." God, for the persona, will always be present in "the remembering and the forgetting," the past *in* the present: "God / in our night, which never can stay night." She cannot hide from God's sun ("Rapture") nor deny the God of History, the glad hand of greeting, its thumb and fingers folding tight into the palm.

Robert A. Fink

Acknowledgments

I am grateful to the editors of the following publications, in which these poems first appeared (some in slightly different versions or with different titles):

Alaska Quarterly Review: "The Jewish Woman Remembers
    Deuteronomy 6:6–9"
Cimarron Review: "How to Make a Jewish Poem," "In Preparation,"
    "Story from Another Inquisition," "The Storytelling Disease"
Crab Creek Review: "The Uptown Lady and the Downtown Woman"
Gigantic Sequins: "Matriarch"
Handsome: "I Don't Know the Story, but I Can Tell the Story"
iArtistas: "The Creation of Temple Beth Sholom"
Kestrel: "The Glass Overcoat"
Linebreak: "First Gentile," "Rapture"
Meridian: "How to Make Yourself Remembered," "Yahrzeit"
Mid-American Review: "*Huevos* for Seder, ix"
MiPOesias: "*Huevos* for Sedar, i-viii"
Musehouse Journal: "The Gossips," "Grandfather Onion"
Poet Lore: "The Joke," "My Sister the Diviner," "Solomon"
RHINO: "My Sister the Abacus"
Witness: "Amidah for Teenage Girls," "Eating Animals without Faces"
The Women's Review of Books: "The Jewish Woman in America, 1941,"
    "The Jewish Woman in America, 2010"

A most heartfelt thank you to Robert A. Fink and the staff of TTU Press for their belief in this collection. I thank Robin Becker and Julia Kasdorf, my teachers and mentors, for their stewardship of these poems in their earliest forms; the most careful readers and dear friends Daniel Story and Sarah Blake; the editors of *AGNI,* for teaching me the literary publishing ropes; my family, for their constant and unconditional support; and Nick, for hearing these same stories a hundred times over and loving me anyway.

The Glad Hand of God Points Backwards

How to Make Yourself Remembered

Bury the trinkets first,
candlesticks or a favorite paring knife,
the silver but not the gold.

If your story has a dog, bury
her bone. In her next life, she'll
return as a woman, find herself
traveling through Germany,
riveted to a patch of ground
in the former West Berlin.

Bury the fragile in a shallow grave—
the cotton skirts, the soft
paper, the white linens
for the Sabbath. Your excavator
should pull your relics whole
from an earth still kind
to its company.

Bury household objects
purposefully to perplex an excavator—
a diaphragm, or an unmarked teaspoon.
That way, when they reconstruct your story,
the little rubber disc will live forever,
an alien saucer, with pins to anchor it
in an American history museum; the spoon
will cradle a weight unasked of it before.

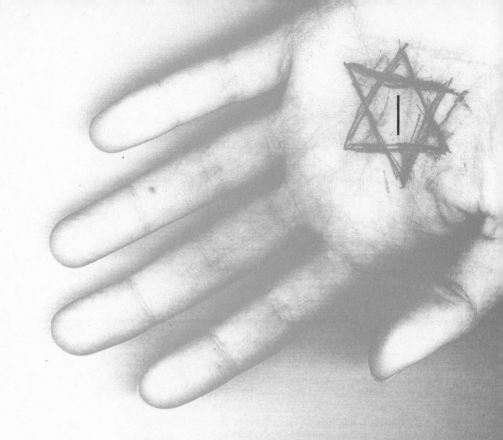

The Glad Hand

Generations back, one Christian woman
converted—her love in a skullcap, prostrate

before something unfathomable.
She yielded thirteen: an American tribe

of doctors and numbers men,
bewildered by the illogic of the Sabbath

candles' glow, God's unscientific tale-telling,
the stories of stories, books

of books, myths of survival, fear untreatable
by sertraline or liquor. Still, their children, we

average a sort of goodness, fill up whole pews
at Friday night services, mouth prayers

old as a thousand matriarchs, made
from symbols of mystery: A, *alef,*

the round hump of *bet,* the cycloptic
pey. We pray together, orderly, to Adam—

that first honorable man,
with as many answers as God,

who watched the earth multiply
with creatures, beautiful as they were dumb.

Matriarch

Sarah had Rebekah had Leah and Rachel had
precedent had sand had order had opposition
had energy had mourning had parchment
and ink had commentary had liturgy had fire had
goats for the altar had the longest dresses
and the longest skirts had offspring had offspring had offspring
had no use for sarcasm but lived thick with God's ironies
had the text of all stories to read to their children at nightfall

had the maps of every city quartered to keep them faithful had
the blessings of a creature more powerful and impulsive had the love
of the men who have loved me or not loved me
had the hearts of the bodies we stand on tall as arks
had the shawl to wrap around my bare and sloping shoulders
had the soil to force into my fists and turn my body west

I see them in Giant Eagle, buying
the same soap and eggs as I buy;
at the Squirrel Hill library,

their sons garbed as God prefers
even in hot July, consoled by the tallit,
trailing blessed white strings

through Forbes Avenue dirt.
The women cover their heads, their skirts
making dark mysteries

of their legs. All faith, they show me
the fabric of inaccessible glory, the rents
in my own life. My God holds

nobody responsible. He lives in the thick air
over Philadelphia, likes it there, doesn't
speak to me much, if at all. My God accepts

the muddle of our lives: reformed,
distracted, desirous of strangers
in other, wilder places. "As you wish," He says,

and retreats into the sunset alone. From Him,
I wrest a path without limits, two strong
and willful legs to bare to a street full of eyes.

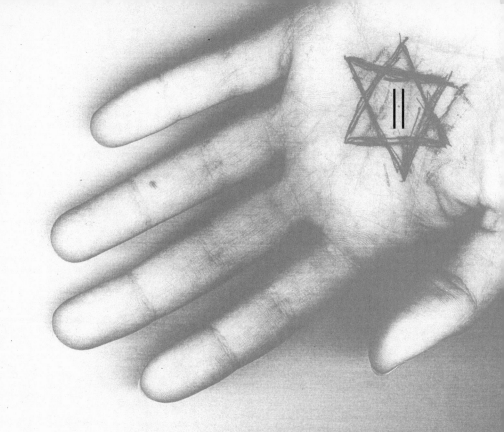

The Glass Overcoat

The scrubwoman works on her knees, hands of lye
and peeling skin: seamstress, home cook,
polisher of silver and gold. Guttural unused German
sticks in the throat like an errant fishbone.
The Jewish immigrant on her knees, sorting
unpacked child's clothes, the apartment
rattling with strange English words—*baseball,
highway, petticoat.* In the dark, a mustard-yellow star
alights coy from the ship-stored garments,
winking at no one. In the window, the Schuylkill
steams and stretches, the city's factories and schools

alive with immigrant sweat. The scrubwoman
dreams at night in German, she flies over oceans,
first a bomb, then a boat. *Das Glas* covers her body,
shards glint like small stars. Days, she's two dollars
for a well-tucked hem, a meal for a washed tile floor.

Schönwetter & Grünewald, Coatmakers

Berlin, 1925

After years of tailoring, Schönwetter
lost all feeling in his fleshy thumbs.
Numbness followed some
thousand pricks of the needle,

a hand practiced at wielding sharps.
At work, Schönwetter's thick brows furrow
at the tiny eye that challenges him
every time he sews.

The machine hums behind him, apprentice's foot
spinning the bobbin onward: through
and through and through goes the thread
in the wool, firm grip of stitch and tug.

A woman stands on a platform
before him, stockinged leg poking
from her thick fox throw. She's ready
for hemming: a quick taking in,

a smart turning under.
Against the floor, the trifold glass
makes storefront words in shadow:
Schönwetter & Grünewald

Schönwetter stitches fur to leather
flush against Gentile skin; he draws thread
on a giant spool through smaller
and smaller spaces.

The Will of God

On a military bus, Grandfather
sits next to Alfred Dreyfus. History
doesn't matter here: like Dreyfus, innocent
prisoner for decades, God is patient,
flexible, willing for strangers to meet on a bus
in any universe. Jewish soldiers
for secular wars, the pair sit swathed in khaki
and steel, somewhere in nowhere France.
Or better: over powdered eggs in Poland, they fiddle

with their caps, their laces, waiting for deployment
to the camps. God, with two hands, could cover
the eyes of both men, if he so desired. Or:
Grandfather finds himself in front of Dreyfus's
grave in Montparnasse, a rose suddenly pressed
in his palm. He knows the words to the Kaddish,
says it reflexively; the tears that come, for this stranger,
belong to God. Or, back on the bus, each man
rubs the corner of impossible photographs—tiny

granddaughters, soft and red. "Look at her,"
Dreyfus says, pointing. "And her," says Grandfather.
Neither finds more words, the future
in front of them smudged, undeniable. The girls,
newborn, screaming for air—the pair can hear them
circling their ears with pain, or is it promise,
that learned search for oxygen, that causes them both
to wring their tired hands, unprepared
to touch babies with their war-ruined palms.

The Glass Overcoat

After Kristallnacht, 1939

Schönwetter's coats shrug, bored on their hangers,
indifferent to the night's red theater:
the warp of his coat racks, his closets of ash.

Today, he learns how clothes betray.
In the wreckage, hundreds of buttons
spring loose, slink away. Dummies, split

down their spines, burst open, revealing
guts of bolts and gears. Old customers pass,
kicking aside findings with a steely toe.

A glass overcoat waits, open
on the sidewalk: sleeves of debris
for his cold arms to slide inside.

From him, I learned to mend. Only
once have I botched my stitches, sewn
a pocket shut, then mistakenly tried

to thrust my hands inside for safety:
hands chapped or soft, who can remember,
open and waiting for the frost.

One by one her mother sold her silver spoons
and heirloom bracelets; goodbye, porcelain bear,
silk blouses, patent-leather Mary Janes, the scarves
and stud earrings for newly pierced ears, the red wool coat
spotted walking on another tiny body's shoulders
down *Wittenbergplatz*. Goodbye, books bound
·in leather, bone china, even the hangers, the goblets
and cabinets; goodbye to the Torah buried in the backyard,

the neighbors, the schoolmates, the mothers dressed so well
at services, the men with businesses who stayed behind
one week, two weeks more. What stylish
objects they became: the coins from fillings
and wedding rings, the soap, the wigs, lamp
after lamp to light a thousand decorated homes.

Frank Lloyd Wright
had built most of his legacy,
and it was good—Fallingwater
tumbled over itself
in Pittsburgh; the Guggenheim perched
on the Upper East Side. Then
the Lord appeared to him
as he lay in bed one night.
The Lord said unto Wright: *Bring*
your pens and your drafting paper
to Philadelphia, where you shall build
a new house of worship
for the Jews.
Wright, Midwest Baptist
minister's son, sat up straight
in bed. *The Jews?* he asked, then pointed
a finger at the ceiling. *What*
do you think my art can bring
to the Jews? The Lord said
unto Wright: *Between you and me:*
I've been a bad father
lately. And thus Beth Sholom,
mountain of glass, giant
winged ark, came to land
on Old York Road, the last building
Wright designed before
his death: forever stuck
in self-reflection, the panes
making walls and roof of sky.

i

Grandfather signed
the ketubbah, looked to God
for His signature. *It's not so easy,*
God said to Grandfather. Pen
in hand, the first wife
shook and shook.

"God won't talk to me," she said to Grandfather.
It's not so easy, God whispered.
What I have done to you, He said.

ii
Here's the truth: Grandfather
loved another woman before
Grandmother, wanted her,
swore to her all that comes
with the covenant—his body

over hers, shield and till.
Her ailing body in bed beside him,
her blood surprised
into his monogrammed handkerchief.

I can tell no more, because the truth
stops here, rests only
with our God, the
collector of stories
and bodies.

iii

It's not so easy, God said
to the American soldier
and his Dachau bride. "God's fingers
are stuck in my ears,"
said the first wife,
"and I cannot hear
a thing." Grandfather and the rabbi
and the first wife stood

at the altar, and together
they were wed.
Above, God kept a humble
distance, knowing
the worth of His promises.

Tailor, doctor, mohel. What do we so badly
want to excise? We make our trade with scissors
and scalpels, tuck hems, sew silk or skin
with equal ease. Walking down the Boulevard,

we fare as well as circus clowns. (Those funny hats,
that curly unruly hair!) And the guilt:
the weight, the backbending weight
of survival. Like a Sabbath candle that's burned

all night, how the wax coats a silver stick, deforms it,
a lumpy Quasimodo. In this world, we cut away
what we cannot hoist onto the shoulders
of our children. We calculate our breaking

point with a hand made for surgery. So many of us
scientists. So few of us evangelists.

Grandfather Onion

The rank one, the sharp one, the one
always in need of other flesh
for company, Grandfather searches for onions,
eats them with every meal. Red shards
in tomatoes, naked but for salt, the yellow ones

sighing pleasurably into schmaltz.
Turned and turned by the spoon
of my grandmother, he fishes them
one half-moon at a time
from the scalding fat barely rendered.

His brittle skin peels. A plume of hair
flies above the taut tan dome of his skull.
Grandfather of the pickled tongue, vinegar
and capered tongue, he drapes lox
the color of surprise on top of onions,

seeking the stink of Jewish food,
its herrings and its livers, its complicated
briny odors, its conversations
between skin and sea. He sheds tears, a matter
of course, another sort of craving: tears for

the stirrer, the learned sting
that comes with marriage, with peeling
back its skin and slicing it deeply. They must
know the lessons of each generation, feel
that thick, stinging pleasure in their eyes.

For Rose

Practical, we take the names of our dead
because the dead are sturdy—stern mantles
of opportunity, watching as we shoulder them
from windowpanes, closets. Rose—one curling *r*

makes hundreds of us, Rachels, Rivkas, Renates,
Richards, Ronalds, this slip of a woman
in a fading photograph keeps all our tongues
moving. Blessed are you, lord of our passed-on,

our looking-over-us-on-high, as the dead name us
consonant, as we cast aside the baby books and run
curious to the headstones, hunting for names
among the mausoleums and weather-worn

statues, the roses gone to pulp beside the roses
freshly brought, red and resonant.

Grandfather Shoemaker

Bodies piled in a truck, bare feet
making cold pyramids. Beside
them: Grandfather, dressed in
wool, American issue, stands rigid

in his polished black boots
that shine with light whose source
cannot be seen. Grandfather sits
at a picnic table in France, food gray

against a gray sky, on his way back
to the States; his muddy rubber rain boots
reach almost to his knees.
In Philadelphia, Grandfather stands proud

beside the single assembly line, leather
pressed and stamped into shoes
box by box. A child, I stand with my mother
at the closet I share with sisters, the shoes

and boots spilling from its mouth, all outgrown
or forsaken. "I don't understand you girls,"
she says, "your need to collect
so much of the same damn *thing*."

Four Thousand Shoes

Ten years ago in the DC museum,
Grandfather and I examine
that dusty pile
of soles and laces, stretching

from floor to ceiling, wall
to wall to wall.
"How the leather's lasted,"
he admires, and reaches out

past the barrier almost
to touch them.
"This here is work
by a craftsman. You don't see shoes

like these anymore."
My eyes low, archiving
my cheap pleather sneakers,
made by machine to fit

all the feet of the world
exactly the same.
The still machines of Europe
beside us in the museum, tamed

for history; the machine of his body,
valves fluttering with overuse.
"No, those will do you no good,"
my grandfather says,

and points down, toward
the re-created train-car floor.
"Terrible plastic things. Let's go
buy you something handsome."

The old sisters spoke with the wild gestures of trapped birds, snared or cooped, their wings working toward an impossible escape. They stood on street corners in Germantown and gesticulated the full span of their arms. They argued over coffee, over books, over the dinner table, food chilled to the temperature of the air. They hewed their beliefs for the sake of debate. Soft-handed and pale-skinned, they lived mostly inside.

They took the trolley to Center City when they were in their twenties, living in Logan with the rest of the refugee Jews. They told wild stories of their childhoods, never explored or questioned. They worked as bookkeepers, secretaries. They went to Girls' High School, classrooms filled with young women speaking foreign tongues, caught and released, caught and released each day, back when men and women were kept separately until marriage, fine china and daily dishware.

The oldest of the three married a soldier (never explored) who loved her dearly (never questioned). When he died his mouth made words that opened her chest like shrapnel. *Tell them whatever you want,* he said, *but I need you to know. I need you to know.* Her hands stayed slack at her side. *Her name was. It was.* She left his bedside and paced a block of Old York Road, north and south, east and west, as if a cage around her kept her close.

Inheritance

You'll wear his shirts, you say. They bunch, tired,
around your shoulders, hem drooping, old man's
hunch on the back of his son. You'll take your widowed mother
to the store. You'll leave her at the synagogue's heavy door.
You'll file all his paperwork. You'll don his bathrobe: there he stands,
wrapped around your body like a shawl. Inside you his heart

beats curious and sick. As a child, deep in your growing heart,
you knew magic before schoolmates' birthdays—not the tired
deception, the rabbits and cards. Your magicians stood
at the ark, wore yarmulkes, giant black-clad men
enchanting you: books became graves, a blood-rubbed door
saved sons, wires blessed made walls. And your mother,

shoulder to stove, showed the other *goyishe* mothers
a different kind of magic: stuffed your heart
with bread and liver, left open the latch on the porch door
for your easy passage through. With her silent math, her untiring
calculus of recipes, she knew the needs of men
who never tire, who, always hungry, eat and eat while standing.

Once you saw them make love while standing up,
your father's arms suspending your mother
in air, unknowingly teaching you the ways of man,
the muffled clapping of heart against heart.
Their days of labor left neither one too tired
to lean precipitous against the bathroom door

and find each other. From the doorway
you thought this an incredible trick, standing
balanced on toes, speaking no language, never tiring.
The next morning, for the first time, your mother
sat at the table in a men's shirt, rubbing that spot above her heart.
You learned, at thirteen, the magic making of a man

who studied Hebrew, sang its script, became God's man,
who shut the Torah inside a heavy wooden door
and pledged himself to God with a flitting heart.
Today, if you pray, you think of those dark men standing
beside your siblings and your beaming mother,
your father whose heart sighed and stopped, utterly tired.

Death turned your father into a candle, a rock that stands
in wind and rain. Death turned your mother into a door
that only opens for strangers, a shirt impossible to rend.

Yahrzeit

Here the eye of God opens, unblinking,
at the throats of our grandmothers. The small pale
candle flickers on the windowsill, making
constellations of all our deaths.

How long a wick, how short a year. And here,
the family site, the only real estate
that's mine—how clever, the way earth
makes us into mud—how heavy

the feet of our commemorators, how white
the knuckles that clasp their books of prayer.

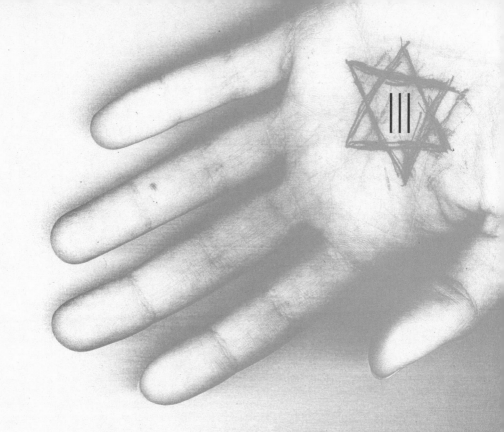

The Book, Open

How to Make a Jewish Poem

What makes this poem Jewish? Nobody's
blessed it yet. Nobody's named it,
named it again in Hebrew, put that name
on a Kiddush cup, filled that cup
with wine purple as a bruise.

Who's going to march it
up and down the aisles,
dress and undress it
like a newborn at the altar,
kiss the book that taps it
from the pews?

Where are the bobby pins to stick
the lace to this poem's crown, cover
its head on the Sabbath? Where's
this poem's sense of ritual? Its litany
of tics, its love of counting?

Let's call this poem Rivka. Also,
Becky. Also, Rose, an ancient
relative this stanza's never met.
Let's yoke it to the ox of rules.
Let's light a candle after dark,

smash a glass under its husband's foot,
circumcise its wailing, red-faced
sons, watch it multiply
into a book (some poems
will remember, some
will not)—sit shivah
for its passing once
it ends.

The Storytelling Disease

I don't think I've ever told you this story before
the one about your father putting our dachshund down the backyard slide
and the poor dog broke his leg

and there was the time way before then in Berlin I went to the Olympics
and had to sit up high with all of the other Jews and the SS they marched
I remember clapping along with your aunt balanced on my knee
     like a stuffed bear

or the story I told you about your grandfather that leaves out the parts
that make me upset and that includes parts that I've added
so you don't ask questions about the rest

what good is storytelling at my age if I can't tell you stories the way
     I want to

I was a bookkeeper with your grandfather's sister and one day
     I rang her bell
and your grandfather answered the door with a towel on his shoulders

when we bought the house on Cheltenham Avenue I pulled up all the
     original shrubs
one bush at a time my hands around the root just to be sure
when you find love you will see marriage is easy if you know the right
     stories to tell

when you've lived something dark and big someone else's stories can mix
     with yours
a documentary or a museum display or another synagogue yenta

once I told you we had to bury our Torah but that might not be true
or maybe you read it in a novel or maybe I just remembered wrong I was
  young then after all

I remember Max that ridiculous dog what kind of God makes animals
  with legs like that anyway

The Uptown Lady and the Downtown Woman

Grandmother says: *marriage is like a bucket.*
In Northeast Philadelphia, gloved and fox-stoled,
she'd prowled for a husband. Today,
the Boulevard fills with mattress stores
and discount bodegas, dirty snow, tenements
the Jews left for Germantown and Merion,
lean men wearing sandwich signs:

Going Out Of Business!, their entire torsos
gone bankrupt. Feeling responsible, prostrate
before her success, Grandmother adopts
servants and housecleaners like strays, her husband
always in the factory, stamping leather soles
for ornate, impractical shoes. The Irish maid
scrubs and scrubs a sparkling tile floor, her

hands in the bucket. *Fill it brimming over,*
lift it to your shoulders, bathe yourself in cold,
refuse your body's shivering wants. Grandmother's
voice from the bedroom: *This was*
my mother's work. I was lucky, she says
as the candlesticks shine, as the roast
darkens, spits and smokes in its tiny hell.

Small planets of gefilte fish,
mashed carp and
pike. The boneyard

around me—ribcages,
still-erect fins and backbones. I've
left them this way, bellies parted

like books at their spines, the pile
of scales, absent shorn skin.
Bent open haggadah, balanced

in one of my grandfather's
manicured hands. The planets
on plates, one world for

each guest. The salt water
still in tiny bowls. The bitter
herb that we eat in unison,

our tongues burning and
twisting. I didn't understand
before why grandmother

wanted our hands on
the bones. We remember
the slaves, fingernails

smelling of the sea. We
use the lost bodies in
the kitchen, boil them

for stock, my sisters
and I standing over
the vat of skeletons

and peeled halved onions,
or forget them,
iridescent waste, crush them

in the trash compactor, the same
mess next year, the cleanest
of hands beginning.

The Joke

Not one for prayer, my father
introduced me to his Judaism:
Mel Brooks' *History of the World,*
Part I. Brooks dons the robes

of Moses, our greatest prophet,
brings us fifteen commandments
and then smashes a tablet onto Sinai stone.
Can you hear me? God asks of Moses.

A deaf man could hear you,
Moses replies—and thus, as God
lets Moses live, God is good
humored. Hitler,

strapped to ice skates, enraptured
by his triple Lutz, never looks
toward the camera, stays faceless,
a snippet of red flashing

from his bicep as he spins.
My father and I clutch
our sides, laugh
until we weep, which isn't

like weeping at all.
Today—a good Jew, my father's
daughter—I can make a joke
out of almost anything.

The terrible world becomes a reel
and I tap-dance in front
when it gets too dark. After a time,
this is what Jews call

being exhausted: my father, his feet
raised, head bent over wine
in front of the television, room
for my child-self to sit

beside him. Together we laugh
in our private bodies
at the breasts, the erections,
the execution jokes,

while Brooks stands
flush against the guillotine,
assures my father: *it's good*
to be the king.

I Learn of Slaughter

Sunday in the supermarket,
all the Kosher meat's expired. I think
of the chicken pulled from its cage, forced
to hear Hebrew as the rabbi sanctifies it, slits

its throat. Last comfort for a surely Jewish
terror: waiting and waiting for a death
that's coming soon, death that we march from or to
in all our liturgical texts, death that's felled so many

from the photo albums, the dinnertime stories—
don't come for us, not yet. When history
says it's time, when we've worn out
our welcome, grown fat from the farmer's

land, lulled by the sweet sound of praising
God, death will come: the knife
so heavy in our neighbor's hand.

Story from Another Inquisition

Deborah wasn't a Jew, and then
she is: one day, the salt from lox—so
flushed, so red—no longer
cloys, but harkens to a parted sea,

a mat of smoke and ocean
on the tongue. Or maybe
a relative in Argentina picks up
the phone, calls Deborah, speaks

the *Barchu* slowly, the Hebrew filling
her ears, unlocking like a door. This relative,
a quiet old refugee Jew, speaks Spanish
to his mailman, but whispers

"I love you" to his wife in Polish each night
before bed—the candlesticks
kept polished in the closet, a habit
of secrets. Maybe Deborah's always been good

at keeping her own secrets—the clarinet
that makes her weep, street-corner Klezmer,
the melody she knew before she came
into existence. She's always felt old, so

old, older than all the graves
of Europe, older than Eve, who,
like all Jews, had to learn the truth
at the site of her hungry mouth.

The Gossips

The women collect around the wine and we talk, we yak
competitively, we stretch hours of living into weeks of dissection,
we perform miracles of chatter, we are mouthy Olympians, in love
with our athleticism. We learned the art from our grandmothers,
who prattled, stirred the deep pot of fat, carcasses piled by the sink.
An educated yenta holds her secrets like currency, spends
one light gold coin at a time—the sins of the neighbor boy revealed
just as the cleaver descends on dinner's wan neck,

just as the boy's mother slips inside to overhear. Our town criers,
our lapsed priests, at their feet we sit, helpless from the tabloid,
begging for the next salty scrap, making our own communes of myth
around plates of cheese, bottles of booze. We fuel up on these
tiny histories. We block out the dirty tired world, its weary beds and
tables. We live in parallel, dwell in the stories we have to learn to tell.

Yahrzeit

Three ropes in the challah, no
lament in the Kaddish,
four corners of the shouldered tallit,
its six hundred and thirteen strands
meticulous in permutation, prime
in rule: a fetish,

a counting. Grandmother alone
at her cluttered boudoir, her back
to the doorway carved by men
now dead, the stones on stone
at Grandfather's grave
in Philadelphia, promised pebbles,

we count them, his children, toss them: they fall
each time back to the earth. We forget
nothing, and inter what returns.
We rip at our breasts the silk
of our sorrow. We shock,
each time, at our softness.

Memory: we learn to braid it into plaits
and bake it for hours. We take it
by the ears and bless it,
grind it to a headstone's polished slick,
bury it on its heaviest side
in the earth.

It goes: Grandmother grabbed me from my mother's grasp
like there had been some sort of error, like the thirty-six hours
of labor and contractions had come from her own long-empty
belly. I was immediately hers. Of course, I remember nothing

from this night. Newest to Earth, I'm held in the mouth
of my family narrative: *she moved quick. She made demands.*
The three of us in the sterile room, the first grandchild a swaddle
of perfect wet rage. The three of us, already lost

to each other. What's given must have its take. To fill arms,
arms must empty. And so my grandmother left my mother
for the longest moment without her first child, opened her reach
to me, who should have fought and only cried, who can summon

not a moment of this fissure, who grew up to write down the truth
and the lies together. Who remembers the future; who reads
     the past first.
Who holds up her hands to be held and, waiting, feels the night.
Who builds the museum before the victor comes to claim her dead.

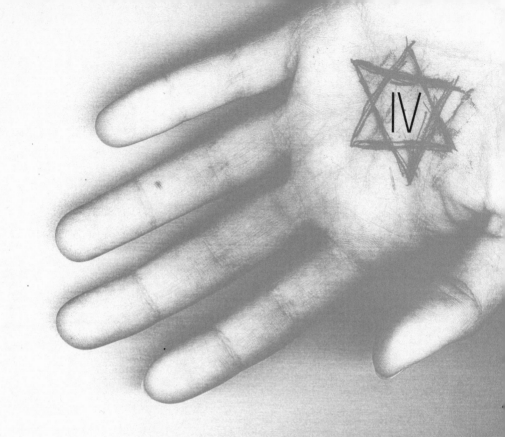

IV

Elijah

Huevos for Seder

i
At home, we'd pray for a good
supper, then set an extra place
at the table for a stranger—
the perfect

guest. Our savior surely
would never eat his eggs
raw, not like *madre*, who drinks
superstitiously from the shell,

breaks them open
with her bare hands, looks
hungrily at the runny life inside.

ii

Map of Europe between us, *madre*
and I sit at her kitchen table.
"You are Jewish?" she asks me. "I'm
American," I say. "You are Jewish,"
she says. (America, invention
of the nomad, roof over the outcast's
head.) "Then I'm German," I say. "No,"
she tells me, kind in her surety. "I am

Spanish. You are Jewish." Thus,
I learn about nationalism:
that unscalable wall, that darkened,
padlocked home. I inherit
the menacing map entire. I live,
lost, in each nation of sand.

iii

In Toledo, the synagogues
are all museums, stamped
and tiled with the crescent and
the cross—a reception hall

for all of Abraham's children.
Whoever had the biggest army
got to pick the decorations. In Madrid,
all Orthodox, they keep a cop outside.

iv
I slurp it raw, the Spanish *huevo*
that lives on the shelf, somehow
never spoils, just as *madre*
taught: *let the yolk*

break on your teeth. It spills
like a prayer from my lips.

V

Easier than I'd thought
to shrug off identity's
warm jacket—it hangs
nicely from the peg

in the *vestíbulo*, draped
with some care,
designed for storms
and squalls but worn only

in sunshine. Under
the jacket: the slow,
naked heart

of shame, same
old matriarch hips,
same balled
matriarch fists.

vi

The men of Spain
have stadium hungers, loud
and exultant. They whistle at us
from street corners, scream
when the *fútbol* player scores,
bring us at night to their parents'
homes through windows
and fire escapes. *She*
wouldn't approve, they say
of their sleeping mothers: their
televisions quiet, their crucifixes
nailed to the wall. Our mothers
still on Eastern Standard time,
constantly living in the past.
Good, we might say: or nothing
at all, taking them
whole and new inside us
like experience.

vii

Beitzah—the egg
at American seder: hardboiled
in its pristine outfit,
left whole to commune

with the lamb shank and the bitter
herb. Smug, it never wobbles
from place. Even boiled,
the egg is commentary: symbol

of a temple's destruction, the taste
of sulfur just as the funeral
ends, the coming of spring.

viii

Pepper or ash: the spots
in our dinner of eggs.
At the stove, ash, ash,
madre Madrileña with

a Lucky Strike in her mouth.
Our eggs taste rich
with the soot, the cook's
cigarettes and our hunger

mashed together on one
fork. We eat them oily,
potatoes fanned throughout
like thin white moons.

Who's to say dirt never
made a meal better, some sour
blackness against the yellow sun, grit
in the gift of sustenance?

ix

After I move to Spain,
three of my friends fall ill—
salmonella. Another friend

finds a cross nailed above her bed
after she wears her Star of David
necklace to the dinner table. I'd left

all my jewelry in America:
could you ever live with yourself
if you lost it, my mother said.

At the *mercado*, an old man sells me misshapen metals. I hold one, lumpy and blank, as expressionless as the back of a stranger's head— maybe at the tail end of a long journey, his hair and neck moles a landscape just barely familiar. "From the War," the old man says. "I can see that you like it." It's a paperweight, he tells me, old bullets melted to a fist of lead, spent rounds from his uniform's pocket, traveled all the way from Germany.

The stranger's head—he's on a train in Germany, the earth rising in black hills to the window. His body of potential shares the train-car air with mine. Together in those seats, we sit perfectly still, we hurtle through the countryside at breakneck speed. Night turns to day, to night. My grandmother appears between us, a quiet child, flame star stitched to her handmade lapels. What is it that I want to say to him, what's almost readable in those thinning hairs? "For your novel?" the old man asks. "Or your important papers. Nice, heavy. So each page, it stays in the right order."

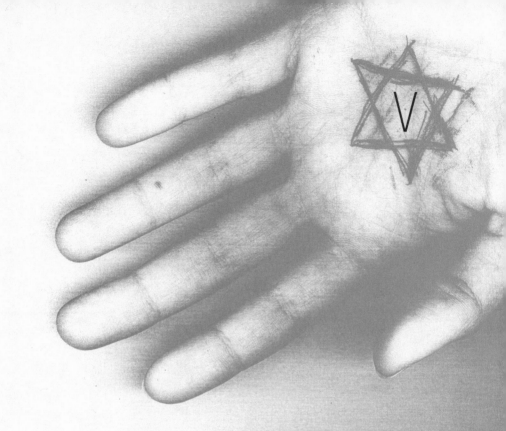

The Jewish Woman
in America

V

Solomon

As children, my sister and I dressed as brides;
the gown in the basement came from anywhere,
hand-me-down, touched any body
before ours. We'd line up in our bedroom,
preen and bat our eyes, say: *I do. I do. I will.*
We married each sort of imaginary man.
We gave these suitors no gifts, took turns
with them: *This one carries the mail. This one
lives in the biggest building in Philadelphia. This one knows
all the words to "Back in the USSR." This one prefers
soccer to football.* Her turn, then mine
to watch the other wed, covered in the found
jewels of our family, dust rising with each breath
inside the ivory. *This one will be Jewish*: my chance
at the altar, veil just pinned. *What other kind of man
is there?* she asked, covering my face.

Amidah for Teenage Girls

We said it Friday nights in unison: *blessed*
is Abraham, Isaac, patriarchs whose weight
we felt against our chests, *Jacob,* whose brother

filled his mouth with the sand of hate,
who split sisters with his body
of patience. *The God of History*, reads

the siddur, nothing more dangerous
than this sort of God. Any good girl
will tell you so: ask Leah, who watched

as her betrothed tilled fields in agony,
rutted at her nightly, his pious bride, as he dreamed
for seven years of younger Rachel's face. God,

our brute teacher. God, whom we thank
and thank for these big men. *You are mighty forever,*
my Lord. You resurrect the dead. My Lord, open

my lips, that my mouth may declare
Your praise. Imagine the shock, that first boy
or man inside us for mere seconds, the tremor

of realization—some smaller God at our clavicle,
thrumming in awareness. *The creator of all things.* And so
when I lie with him, my body already knows what to do

while he shifts his weight, moves his hips. *You cause*
the wind to blow and the rain to fall. The hard ram's horn,
the arms thrust high, parting a sea of salt. *O King,*

•

helper, savior and shield. And what of our
pleasure, that quiet subtext, that patient search against
our partners' sweaty brows, near to finished? We already

know the phrase: *bestow, bestow.*

How to Make a Jewish Marriage, 1949

Beware the grinding fist, the blanched knuckle, the outstretched hand.
Beware the man who takes any girl's face between his hands.

The laughing man—greet him with your entire self. Take him
patiently, but take him: his want makes an open, flattened hand.

Ride his wishes to his parlor; ride his hopes to your hopes.
Ride in the driver's seat when he's away. Grip the wheel
        in your white-gloved hands.

Wash your hair, watch your waist, scrub your limbs and creases
        clean each night.
No one should know what you've touched just by looking at your hands.

Amnesiac, you become American. Historian, you remain a Jew.
        Your story
begins: the book open like supplicant palms. Strike your words
        with an exacting hand.

First Gentile

I promise him bitterness, salt,

               the tastes of all my dead, gold and wax,
the roots of trees. Against me, he is

               scaffolding, linen, bicep and thigh, all
newness: private liturgy of high school hunger,

               snow collecting on his parents' car.

I've just observed Hanukah, the consecrated

               fuel that burned on faith,
young enough to believe in the miracle

               that's mine alone: a forsaken fuse
and the hands that light it,

               the labor of soldiers and battle
and cold, then the flame. He finds me

               in handfuls—first hair, then skin,
then cries, then silence, his torso

               reclothed, tying his sneakers.

"You'd be better at this," he says—

               at touching so quickly, efficient and practiced
—"if you stopped thinking so much."

               But I have the worries of my great-aunts,
their consonant names.

               After he leaves, the snow melts
to puddles, the engine of my mouth

               runs on the fumes of God.

To Those Still Godless

This is how your gut makes want. This is how
your body drives. You're left to reckon the mess
yourself. Vanity, you learn, is thinking yourself

some sort of god. You might look in your full-length
mirror and think—*I know who made this. I see the creature
who made me ready for wanting.* And, so taken,

you shutter your parents' house of lessons, you write your myths
on the backs of your lusts, you kiss in alleyways, parks,
hot in the homes of strangers, proper slaves to the seats

of your power. You follow the eyes of the eyes
that survey you, wish to see what they seek, know their
satisfaction. You learn the grinding gears of your

desire. You learn nothing, blotted by orgasm, and hunt again.
Feel that, there, with your tongue or finger: the ridge
where the mouth's roofed canyon goes from soft to hard. Chase that

predetermined transition, the bridged and unfixable chasm
where God made us all identical. Bolt after it, fast
as you can, every day. The rest of your young life.

Bulimia has made my sister visionary—
        "Tomorrow," she says to me, "will be
a better day." And there she sits: an oracle.
        This is how Romulus founded Rome.
Their bowls of organs, their scrambling
        soothsayers, counting to six or twelve.
Their hands in the guts, rummaging for answers.
        Their surety in the process. Their results.
Two fingers, hard at work pressing
        down, down. Beside her bent back I sit,
waiting, my temples pressed against her kidneys.
        Tomorrow, at the breakfast table,
we'll open the *Times,* read of nations
        waxing and waning, all plot. Love
keeps us together at the table, feasting on eggs
        and bread and butter—love, that closed mouth,
fit always, despite ourselves, to bursting.

How Will You Raise Your Children?

Abraham or Abraham, spring
feast or spring fast? In what tongue
must you pray, Hebrew
or Latin? Do your holy men

anoint babies with water
or knives? Do you bless the wine
for the prophet coming or the prophet
gone? Where is the sun when

you bless the wine for the prophet
coming or the prophet gone?
Which fetish did your great-great-
grandfathers teach your great-

grandfathers, to sign
the cross or to pin
the yarmulke? Whose fetish
will live on in their tiny hands; who

will guide them through the air?
Will you lead down
the path of your certainty
with the left foot of day

or the left foot of night? And what
of us? The ones who mourn
a change, then change;
the ones who must.

My Sister the Abacus

In high school, she says,
          the hallways make a perfect
alien music: eight hundred
          and six slamming

lockers, her feet stuck in place
          until they all reply
in kind. She taps and taps in
          air, she makes a calculus

of her fear; her own
          actuary, she takes
no risk and imagines hundreds; she
          cradles her research

against her chest, the angles
          checked and checked
again, the circle drawn exact,
          the silence inside gaping—O, O

—zeroes after two on the red-
          numbered clock, the tires that spin
on winter ice. She says:
          I'm taking Honors Psychology

this year. Exactly one hundred
          and seventy-four miles
northwest, I hear her twist
          and twist our home phone's

thick black cord, nervous laugh
          like an adult. I'm learning a lot
about the human brain, she
          says: orbital-frontal, the loop

•

that swings between the thalamus
        and the caudate nuclei.
Serotonin, uptake, reuptake.
       I think I have one

of the following disorders,
        she says, I made a list,
are you ready to hear them?
        do you have a pen handy?

Eating Animals without Faces

The kashrut teaches us: eat only from what we can stare
straight in the eye, mix it with nothing, feel its throat between
　　　two prayerful

hands. What we hide from is evil: boiled alive, shell-entombed
and silent. The mussel, bland and fat as a tongue—or the scallop,
　　　the clam,

the conch, storied for its powers of arousal. All the ocean flotsam
of the world, culled onto the sand in giant purges, the sea prepared

to answer our strange urges, all sorts of basal hungers. What we seek
alone at night stays hungry, always hungry, your chest

against my back, rocking like a lost boat in a storm. Your face
roots at the nape of my neck, all animal, impossible to see.

Tell me, you whom I love so well;
Where do you pasture your sheep?

Song of Songs 1:7

Marrying a Christian, she feels like a sheep
stuck on some ancient hill. The field quakes
with her ancestors' crusade.

She calls to Abraham, faith's
shepherd, to drag her love
and her away. They shout *Abraham!*

with equal weight in both
their prayerful mouths. Their tribesmen count
the flock apart—as *hers*, as *his*.

Rapture

Wet pink shock of a sliced-open
peach, pit hard between our teeth,
reached in a liquid, honest hurry.
Peach in the fingers of a certain lover's hand.
Peach juice sliding down the wrist of a man
with assertive hungers. Peach, bringer
of rapture: the climax, but not
the fall. Peach sky rising up and up, free
of consequence. Impossible, but for
our chase of it. Peach in the crisper drawer,
softening. We hear stories of the pastor
and his book, so certain of fire, his biblical
calculus. Peach hot, sugared in an oven.
The mouth of red around the brain-
shaped, dumbstruck stone. Peach the very taste
of sin. Peach that sends the crows circling,
rapture here and gone. Peach God, rapt for carrion,
turning above us in the heavens, waiting for
us, ripening, to satisfy ourselves;
come to him pitted, come to him
finished, made rotten by
your sweet time in his sun.

The Jewish Woman Remembers Deuteronomy 6:6–9

We cry for God in worship, later
in bed, witness to the power of giving
up our power. Outside, the wind

crying for God, outside
in the fit of rain a God
just forming. Our bodies

naked before men are God, as sure
as the force that pushes men
toward and toward us, what they search

for is a noise in the earth
like God growing crops, still saving
room enough for the cemeteries.

The lungs expand with our God, God
in the scream, also the moan.
In the splitting of wood and the spilling

of blood, the slaughtered bull and the
dismounted horse. God of the summoning
curling finger. The broken limb

and its setting right. God in
the remembering and the forgetting,
the sheepskin paper and the pulp. The words

we can recite, their loosening as we
walk to our end—God, that keeps our eyes
reading. God in the hands that close

the book, remove the spectacles,
and turn off the light. God
in our night, which never can stay night.

alef the first letter of the Hebrew alphabet.

Barchu recited at every morning and evening service, the prayer that introduces the main part of the synagogue services.

bet the second letter of the Hebrew alphabet.

Amidah prayer giving thanks to the Talmudic patriarchy—Abraham, Isaac, and Jacob.

beitzah the roasted egg placed on the Passover seder plate.

haggadah liturgical text used during the Passover holiday. At Passover seder, the guests read through the entire text, which tells the story of the enslavement and freedom of the Jews in Egypt.

Kaddish the prayer customarily recited by Jewish mourners. The Kaddish makes no mention of death; instead, it praises God and speaks to God's greatness, asking mourners to do the same.

kashrut the Jewish dietary laws that govern the keeping of a kosher household. In a kosher home, meat and dairy must never be mixed on the same plates or at the same meal. The eating of pork and shellfish is also expressly forbidden.

ketubbah a historically Jewish marriage "contract" traditionally outlining the groom's duties in respect to the caretaking of his bride. Both bride and groom sign and choose witnesses to the marriage. The ketubbah must be displayed in the home, and usually contains artfully drawn images or designs.

Kiddush the Hebrew blessing recited over wine, often also involving a Kiddush cup, a ritual glass that holds the wine for the blessing.

mohel a rabbi specially trained to perform circumcisions.

pey the seventeenth letter of the Hebrew alphabet.

seder the traditional ceremonial dinner held during the Passover holiday. The centerpiece of the seder table is a seder plate that displays special foods symbolic of the holiday (see *beitzah).*

shivah the initial seven-day period of mourning that follows the burial of a loved one in Jewish tradition.

siddur Sabbath prayerbook, used during the weekly observation of the Sabbath.

tallit traditional prayer shawls worn by men inside the synagogue and woven from 613 strands, one for each of God's commandments to the Jews, according to the Torah. The strands are then knotted ritually at each end into fringe called *tzitzit.*

Torah the most sacred book of the Jewish people, beginning with the creation of the world in Genesis and ending with Deuteronomy and the death of Moses. It contains much of the history and traditions of the Jewish people.

yahrzeit meaning literally a year's time, it is the anniversary of a death, in accordance with the Jewish calendar. In Orthodox Judaism, visits to the grave and to the synagogue take place, as well as fasting. The family in observation also lights a yahrzeit candle after sundown the evening before the death's anniversary.

yarmulke (also *kippah)* a small, round head covering worn as a symbol of respect and religious observance in a synagogue.

Rachel Mennies is also the author of the chapbook *No Silence in the Fields* (Blue Hour Press, 2012). Her poems have appeared in *Hayden's Ferry Review, Poet Lore, Indiana Review, DIAGRAM, Black Warrior Review, Sycamore Review*, and other literary journals, and have been reprinted at *Poetry Daily*. Born in the Philadelphia area, she lives in Pittsburgh and teaches in the First-Year Writing Program at Carnegie Mellon University.

Selected by Robert A. Fink, *The Glad Hand of God Points Backwards* is the twenty-third winner of the Walt McDonald First-Book Competition in Poetry. The competition is supported generously through donated subscriptions from *The American Scholar, The Atlantic Monthly, The Georgia Review, Gulf Coast, The Hudson Review, The Massachusetts Review, Poetry, Shenandoah,* and *The Southern Review.*